HOMOSEXUALITY
A NEW CHRISTIAN ETHIC

HOMOSEXUALITY: A NEW CHRISTIAN ETHIC

Elizabeth R. Moberly

JAMES CLARKE & CO
Cambridge

James Clarke & Co. Ltd
P.O. Box 60
Cambridge CB1 2NT
England

British Library Cataloguing in Publication Data
Moberly, Elizabeth R.
    Homosexuality: a new Christian Ethic
    1. Homosexuality—Religious aspects—Christianity
    I. Title
    261.8'35766
    BR 115.H6
    ISBN 0-227-67850-8

First published 1983
Reprinted 1985, 1986, 1988, 1989, 1993

Printed in Great Britain by
The Guernsey Press Co. Ltd, Guernsey, Channel Islands.

PREFACE

The present study attempts to correlate the insights of psychology and of theology, in order to suggest what healing can mean for the homosexual and how it may be achieved. It is based on eight years' work in this area. My hope is that it will promote increased understanding and a wider and more compassionate involvement.

I am grateful to Lucy Cavendish College, Cambridge, for the award of Guest Membership while I wrote this book. A number of friends have supported this work, especially in prayer, and I should particularly like to mention the Revd Clyde and Mrs Rae Whitney; the Revd Roy and Mrs Barbara Barker; Martin Hallett; and the late Fr Lev Gillet, archimandrite of the Orthodox Church, who constantly urged and encouraged me to do this work. As ever, the responsibility for the opinions here expressed must rest with the author alone.

Elizabeth R. Moberly
Cambridge 1982

CONTENTS

1
WHAT IS HOMOSEXUALITY?

In the present state of the debate about homosexuality one thing that seems clear — in an issue renowned for unclarity and difference of opinion — is that two fundamentally incompatible positions continue to be held tenaciously. The one asserts that homosexual acts are legitimate, the other that they are not. Despite the complexity of the overall issue and the various attempts at reassessment, there remains a basic polarisation of opinion over this central issue, which would seem incapable of resolution. It is, however, possible to argue that we have been presented with a false dichotomy. By focussing on sexual expression we have narrowed the scope both of our question and of any possible answer to our question.

Traditionally, Christian thought has drawn a clear distinction between the homosexual orientation and its expression in homosexual activity. Only the latter has been condemned, whether in scripture or in subsequent Christian pronouncements. It is unfortunate that this significant and useful distinction has been reduced to a preoccupation with the status of homosexual acts. It will be contended here that the traditional distinction is due for a reassessment, and in far more positive terms than has previously been the case. What is the type of personality structure that underlies the possibility of homosexual behaviour? To define the former in terms of the presence or absence of the latter tells us almost nothing, yet this is precisely the mistake of much contemporary thinking on the matter. The debate has not yet gone far enough. What is needed, with the aid of contemporary psychological insights, is to explore further what the homosexual condition is *in itself*. Only on such a basis shall we be able to set out our ethical evaluations more clearly and helpfully.

The following interpretation will be based on an independent evaluation of the traditional psychoanalytic position. It will take the view that a homosexual orientation does not depend on a genetic predisposition, hormonal imbalance, or abnormal learning processes, but on difficulties in the parent-child relationship, especially in the earlier years of life. At the same time it will reassess the conclusions traditionally drawn from the evidence of psychoanalysis.

It is sometimes asserted that analytic evidence and explanations are too varied to be helpful. It might be truer to say that the phenomenon of homosexuality is more complex and many-faceted than might at first sight be apparent. From amidst a welter of details, one constant underlying principle suggests itself: that the homosexual — whether man or woman — has suffered from some deficit in the relationship with the parent *of the same sex*; and that there is a corresponding drive to make good this deficit — through the medium of same-sex, or 'homosexual', relationships.

In speaking of a deficit, it must be stressed that this does not always imply wilful maltreatment by the parent in question, as distinct from unintentional or accidental hurt. But in every case, it is postulated, something of a traumatic nature, whether ill-treatment, neglect or sheer absence, has in these particular instances led to a disruption in the normal attachment. This in turn implies that psychological needs that are normally met through the child's attachment to the parent are left unfulfilled, and still require fulfilment.

No parent of a homosexual should necessarily blame himself or herself on account of this disruption in attachment. This must be emphasised in a question where the allocation of responsibility is a particularly complex one. Sometimes there will be direct culpability. If a father makes little effort to find time for his son, or belittles him, or ill-treats him in some way, there is a risk of some form of psychological damage to the child, and the father may be considered to be at fault. But psychological damage need not stem from deliberate ill-treatment alone. A divorce may, in some instances, damage a child's relational capacity in this way, without the parents wanting this to happen (though there may be some varying degree of indirect responsibility here). Above all, early separation or parental absence at a crucial point in the child's development, may in some instances, have long-term negative effects, even if the separation was unavoidable or for good reasons, for instance on account of the illness and hospitalisation of either the child or the parent. In such instances, perhaps no-one can be held culpable. The human situation is such that hurt may sometimes occur without it being a matter for blaming anyone.

The causation of homosexuality is not a simple matter, and several points need to be made in connection with this. One is that many things are capable of causing the disruption in attachment that underlies the homosexual condition. It is not a question of one particular cause leading of necessity to one particular effect. Any incident that happens to place a particular strain on the relationship between the child and the parent of the same sex is potentially causative. At the same time, the effect need not always be actualised. A child may genuinely 'get over' a hurtful situation. Or, alternatively, other damage may result rather than a disruption in the child's attachment to the same-sex parent. It is considerations such as these that make the discussion of causation a complex one. A divorce, for instance, may sometimes have a lasting effect on the child's ability to relate to a parental figure of the same sex; it may affect the ability to relate to a parental figure of the opposite sex; it may have neither effect. This does not imply inconsistency, but simply, and very importantly, the absence of determinism. No particular incident must inevitably disrupt the attachment to the same-sex parent. But any of a wide variety of incidents may, in certain cases, happen to result in this particular form of psychological damage. The common factor in every case is disruption in the attachment to the parent of the same sex, however it may have been caused.

Whatever the particular incident may be, it is something that has been experienced as hurtful by the child, whether or not intended as hurtful by the parent. The parent may or may not be culpable, but in either case the child has genuinely been hurt. The difficulty arises when such hurt is accompanied by an unwillingness to relate any longer to the love-source that has been experienced as hurtful. This implies an abiding defect in the child's relational capacity. The tragedy is that subsequent to this effect the behaviour of the same-sex parent becomes irrelevant, since the child is no longer able to relate normally to him or her. Even if love is offered, it cannot be received. This is crucial both to the statement of the problem and to the question of responsibility.

At the same time it must be emphasised that this relational defect may not be evident, or not more than partially evident, to appearances. At the conscious level an adjustment may be made that leaves few or even no signs of disturbance. The family relationships of a homosexual may in a number of instances seem to be good, indeed, in such cases they are good at a certain level. This is not an objection to the present hypothesis, since what we are speaking of is intrapsychic damage at a deep level, much of which may not be overt or conscious. Similarly, it may not always be readily evident what led to the deficit in the first place. The cause may not always be readily recognised, or recognised for what it is. It is perhaps more surprising how often the difficulty and the cause of the difficulty are obvious.

One-parent families do not necessarily have a higher risk of incidence of homosexuality in the children. On the contrary, one notable study of male homosexuals indicates that only a small group had no father (Bieber *et al.*, 1962). Moreover, sometimes it will be the parent of the opposite sex who is missing; or the death or departure of the same-sex parent may come only relatively late in the child's process of growth; or the absence of a same-sex parent may not result in this particular kind of psychological deficit; or acceptable parent-substitutes may be found. One may contrast children who are overtly deprived of the care of a parent with what might perhaps be termed 'hidden orphans'. These are the children of two-parent families who are no longer able to relate normally to one or other parent, and hence are unable to receive parental care even if the parent in question is present and offers care.

Incidentally, there is no reason to expect that all the children of the same parents will be affected in the same way. What we are speaking of is not a general similarity of environment, but specific difficulties in individual relationships. More than one child may sometimes happen to experience such difficulties, but this need not happen and often it does not.

A point that needs to be made is that there may be a deterioration in the parent-child relationship after the parent discovers that the child is homosexual. It is sometimes assumed that this implies that homosexuality is not caused by relational difficulties in the first place. However, if the original disruption in attachment was followed by an adjustment at the conscious level, it is not surprising that overt difficulties do not appear until later on. More importantly, what we are saying here is not that homosexuality is an independent entity or condition *caused by* difficulties in the parent-child relationship. Rather, the homosexual condition is itself a deficit in the child's ability to relate to the parent of the same sex which is carried over to members of the same sex in general.

Needs for love from, dependency on, and identification with, the parent of the same sex are met through the child's attachment to the parent. If, however, the attachment is disrupted, the needs that are normally met through the medium of such an attachment remain unmet. Not merely is there a disruption of attachment, but, further, a defensive detachment. This resistance to the restoration of attachment (in analytic terms, counter-cathexis and not the mere withdrawal of cathexis) is what marks the abiding defect in the person's actual relational capacity, that long outlasts the initial occasion of trauma. However, the repression of the normal need for attachment has to contend, like every repression, with the corresponding drive towards the undoing of repression — in this case, the drive towards the restoration of attachment. It is here suggested that it is precisely this reparative urge that is involved in the homosexual impulse, that is, that this impulse is essentially motivated by the need to make good earlier deficits in the parent-child relationship. The persisting need for love from the same sex stems from, and is to be correlated with, the earlier unmet need for love from the parent of the same sex, or rather, the inability to receive such love, whether or not it was offered.

This defensive detachment and its corresponding drive for renewed attachment imply that the homosexual condition is one of *same-sex ambivalence*. Love for the same sex is only one side of this phenomenon, and it is a serious mistake to isolate the love-need from the defensive manoeuvre that has shaped it and caused it to persist unmet. The homosexual condition is in fact twofold, and implies a psychodynamic conflict (not necessarily overt or obvious) between the two sides of the ambivalence, the negative and the positive. Basically, this is an avoidance-approach conflict. The attraction involved in the need for attachment has to contend with the aversion involved in the defensive detachment. Thus, depending on whichever side of the ambivalence is the more prominent, the homosexual may for instance experience authority problems (one manifestation of the defensive detachment) or dependency problems (one manifestation of the drive for attachment).[1] The contrast here is not between different types of deficit but between different aspects of one and the same psychodynamic structure. It is this same-sex ambivalence which we would take to be the essence of the homosexual condition in both the male and the female. The only difference would be one of greater or lesser degree in individual cases.

Without going into extensive technical detail, it will nevertheless be helpful to document this hypothesis further. This overall structure of ambivalence involves various distinct components. Firstly, and perhaps most surprisingly, the defensive detachment from the same-sex parental love-source will be marked by hostility, whether overt or latent, towards parental figures and towards other members of the same sex. This hostility may be a component of actual sexual relationships (Fenichel, 1945). In one major study of male homosexuals, it is noteworthy that where the man's father had been hostile to his son, as distinct from merely neglectful or ambivalent, the homosexual partner was invariably identified with the father who had been hated and feared (Bieber et al., 1962). Alternatively, hostility may be expressed in the form of antagonism towards colleagues of the same sex (Barnhouse, 1977); in a marked tendency towards 'injustice-collecting', or fault-finding and the accumulation of resentment (Bergler, 1961); or in authority problems (Ovesey, 1969). In all these instances the unresolved animosity that was originally a response to hurtful behaviour, whether deliberate or unintentional, by the parent of the same sex, has been generalised and has the potential for reactivation in any interpersonal transaction with members of the same sex.

The negative side of the ambivalence may happen to become apparent in adult life, but it must be remembered that it is not an adult manoeuvre as such. Rather, it marks the re-emergence of the child's repressed defensive response. This may to some extent 'latch onto' realistic grounds for complaint in the present, but it is essentially fuelled and motivated by the hurts of the past. It is not for this reason to be dismissed as imaginary, but it is anachronistic, allowing the present to be unreasonably conditioned by the past. At the same time, it is not the projection of unaccepted facets of one's own character, but a transference — the reactivation of genuine interpersonal difficulties, carried over from the relationships of the past to those of the present.

A defensive detachment from the parent of the same sex also implies blocking of the normal identificatory process. This may in some instances, but by no means in all, be expressed in effeminacy in the male homosexual and quasi-masculinity in the female homosexual. An identity is the end-product of a process of identification. Disruption in the latter implies some degree of impairment in the former, though in many instances the sense of identity will be viable even if incomplete. The important point to note is that we are not here suggesting any genuine identification with the opposite sex, but rather a 'dis*identification from the same sex, as one of the implications of disruption in the attachment to the parent of the same sex.

The well-known 'mother fixation' of the male homosexual, which has been a standard ingredient of psychoanalytic theory from Freud onwards, strikes the present writer as being an effect rather than a cause. To be attached to one's mother is in itself entirely normal. However, if there is a defensive detachment from the father, the only remaining channel for attachment is that to the mother. What is normal when complemented by a father-attachment becomes abnormal when isolated from this. But it is only the fact of this isolation that is abnormal, not the attachment as such. Thus, the so-called 'mother fixation' in the male implies, not an abnormal attachment to the opposite sex, but an abnormal detachment from the same sex. At the same time, it is possible for the one-sidedness of this mother attachment to be resented and this may manifest itself in authority problems vis-a-vis the opposite sex. This is, however, secondary to the defensive detachment from the same sex. The homosexual's primary and central defensive barrier, and difficulty in relating, is towards the same sex and not the opposite sex.

Detachment implies that the needs which are normally

fulfilled through the medium of an attachment remain unmet. At the same time, there is a reparative drive towards the restoration of attachment, and hence towards the meeting of unfulfilled needs for love, dependency and identification. In the woman this is the search for a mother-substitute to make up for previous deficits in mothering, whether or not this is consciously realised to be the goal of the relationship. The mother-daughter character of the lesbian relationship has received repeated mention in psychoanalytic literature (e.g. Fenichel, 1945: Storr, 1964: Socarides, 1968). However, this search for a mother-figure is misunderstood if seen as an abnormal attachment. Rather, it is the attempt to resolve an abnormal detachment. The restoration of attachment is not itself the problem, but rather the solution to the underlying problem.

Likewise, in the male homosexual there is a search to fulfil hitherto unmet needs through the medium of a restored attachment. The fact that this is the quest to resume and complete the identificatory process is particularly apparent when virile partners are sought for the sake of obtaining a 'shot' of masculinity through identification with the partner (Socarides, 1968).

The reparative drive seeks to fulfil needs that are normally met through the medium of the child's attachment to the parent of the same sex. In this sense, the homosexual love-need is essentially a search for parenting. However, in many cases this is not the conscious goal of a same-sex relationship; and the same-sex partner need not be an overt parent-figure. Indeed, even in such cases where the partner is a parent-figure, the latter himself has similar needs for parenting. Moreover, the need for parenting will vary from person to person according to the degree of the need. The central factor in all cases is that needs that should have been met through the parent-child attachment, remain yet to be met. What the homosexual seeks is the fulfilment of these *normal* attachment needs, which have *abnormally* been left unmet in the process of growth. At the same time, it should be remembered that we are still speaking of the homosexual condition, and not its translation into sexual activity. The psychological needs of the homosexual are often expressed sexually, but these needs exist independently of sexual expression. A good non-sexual relationship with a member of the same sex is another means of fulfilling such needs. The reparative drive is an essential aspect of the homosexual condition as such, and it is vital to remember this.

This overall structure of same-sex ambivalence *is* the homosexual condition. However, this does not imply that the total structure will be readily apparent in all cases or at all times. Much of it may remain latent, as an unconscious psychodynamic factor. Either side of the ambivalence, positive or negative, may be predominant. The homosexual love-need or reparative drive may often be the only overt or conscious manifestation of this total structure. While the defensiveness vis-a-vis the same sex remains in repression, a renewed attachment may be, and often is formed. However, because the negative side of the ambivalence persists as a dynamic force, even if below the level of consciousness, this means that the reparative attempt may at any time be thwarted by the re-emergence of this defensiveness. Attachment may yet again give way to detachment; the relationship may be subject to instability and disruption. Alternatively, the negative side of the ambivalence may express itself in more general ways, as already suggested.

Either side of the ambivalence may be in evidence, and it is important to remember that these are not separate phenomena, but the two sides of one condition. Either side may be overt or latent; or both may be overt, in which case the possibilities of tension and conflict are more marked; or, in some instances, neither side may be overt. Of its very nature, a case where both sides of the ambivalence are latent is not readily observable. However, in a number of instances it is clear that the emergence of some aspect of the ambivalence has been preceded by a period of general latency. And it is known that some of the hostility to homosexuals arises in persons who are unaware of or unable consciously to acknowledge the presence of homosexual inclinations within themselves.

The predominance of one or other side of the ambivalence may also express itself in other ways. One of these is the presentation of identity. The effeminacy of some male homosexuals and the quasi-masculinity of some female homosexuals is a concrete representation of the defensive detachment from the person's own sex, where the process of same-sex identification has been checked at an early point of development.

Similarly, a marked preference for the company of one or other sex can be an indication of the dominance of either the positive or the negative side of the ambivalence. A male homosexual who habitually prefers female company is giving expression to the often unconscious drive away from his own sex, that is the defensive detachment, whereas the reparative drive is predominant in a male homosexual who prefers male company. In the same way, a female homosexual who especially seeks male company is giving expression to the drive away from her own sex, while the preference for female company marks the reparative drive within her.

The homosexual condition may thus express itself in various ways, since the overall structure of same-sex ambivalence is many-faceted. It has social as well as sexual manifestations, and homo-emotional behaviour can be seen quite apart from sexual activity. Pre-heterosexual relating is by no means simply a capacity for loving the same sex, but a whole gamut of ways of relating both to the same sex and the opposite sex. Vis-a-vis the same sex, there may be any attitude ranging from positive to negative, that is from the reparative drive on the one hand to some expression of the defensive detachment on the other hand. Vis-a-vis the opposite sex, there may be an attempt to seek such company, but, as this is pre-heterosexual, it marks unease in relating to the same sex. One must speak of this as a flight from the same sex rather than as a positive seeking of the opposite sex. Alternatively, the homosexual may feel unease in relating to the opposite sex. This is hardly surprising, since the same-sex identificatory process has not yet been completed, and hence a relationship with the same sex remains the primary psychological need of the homosexual.

In all instances, the homosexual condition is one of same-sex ambivalence. At the same time, one may speak of a homosexual spectrum, in the sense that the deficit involved will vary in degree from person to person. In some instances both the defensive barrier and the corresponding unmet needs will be very marked. In other instances there will be lesser degrees of both these sides of the same-sex ambivalence.

It is where the deficit is less marked that one is likely to find the bisexual. To the extent that same-sex love is still needed, the person is homosexual, and the psychodynamic structure here is the same as in all homosexuality, varying only in degree. True bisexuality implies a greater degree of fulfilment of same-sex attachment needs, prior to defensive detachment, than in most homosexuals. A number of homosexuals may be capable of at least a minimal heterosexual performance, but this does not of itself merit the label of bisexuality. A married homosexual is not necessarily a bisexual, and indeed is not bisexual if his or her chief emotional needs are for the same sex.

At the other extreme of the spectrum is the person in whom the same-sex relational deficit is extremely marked. The ability to relate normally to the parent of the same sex was damaged at a very early age, and hence the normal process of physiological growth has been accompanied by very little of the normal corresponding psychological growth. As this same-sex detachment implies a blocking of the identificatory process, the effects on identity may well be marked when the same-sex deficit is particularly severe. A defensive detachment from the same sex implies *dis*identification: not just an absence of identification, but a reaction against identification. It is here suggested that this process accounts not merely for the whole of the homosexual spectrum, but also for the person who is known as the transsexual.

If radical disidentification has taken place, it is hardly surprising that some people do not feel themselves to be members of their own anatomic sex. The sense of gender dislocation is not imaginary, but entirely realistic, if physiological growth has not been accompanied by the requisite psychological growth. This is not a denial of physiology, but an accurate statement of tragic psychological reality. It is the fact of missing growth, not the awareness of this fact, that is unfortunate. One's own self-image is dependent on identification with the same sex, and the radical checking of the identificatory process results in a correspondingly marked deficit in the actual identity. The aversion from attachment to, and identification with, the same sex here manifests itself in an apparent sense of belonging to the opposite sex. This cross-gender position presupposes a defensive anti-masculinity or anti-femininity in the underlying personality structure. It is not a true cross-gender identity. However, neither is there a true same-sex identity. The absence of same-sex identity is quite genuine.

Transsexualism is not, however, a rationalisation of homosexuality. It marks the extreme end of the homosexual spectrum, but precisely because the same-sex deficit is so marked, it is proper to speak of actual gender dislocation. Most homosexuals do not wish for gender reassignment, because in them the same-sex deficit is not so marked. There would be some overlap between homosexuality and transsexualism, that is to say some homosexuals may suffer from a marked degree of same-sex deficit, whether or not this defensive detachment expresses itself in a demand for gender reassignment. But not all homosexuals are transsexuals, because in them there are lesser degrees of same-sex deficit. It is being suggested, however, that transsexualism in both sexes has the same psychodynamic structure as homosexuality. The difference is essentially one of degree, not of kind. Transsexualism is the most marked degree, but far more commonly homosexuality implies a lesser degree of same-sex deficit. However, insofar as the process of same-sex identification-through-attachment has been checked, homosexuality does itself — in greater or in lesser degree — mark a problem of gender identity.

Transsexualism is obviously an identity problem. As the extreme degree of same-sex ambivalence, it is also a problem of a marked degree of defensive detachment and correspondingly extensive unmet needs. Freud (1911) suggested a link between psychosis and (latent) homosexuality. Here it is being suggested that this link, when it occurs, is but the extreme example of the same-sex ambivalence that constitutes the homosexual condition. All homosexuality involves a defensive manoeuvre, not against homosexual impulses as such, but against attachment to the same-sex love-source. This defensive detachment results in an unmet love-need which, when it re-emerges, is known as homosexual. The defensive barrier may often be relatively minor, but at the extreme end of the spectrum it may be expected to be very marked. It is hypothesised that so-called psychosis is none other than the re-emergence from repression of the extreme form of this defensive barrier. Thus, in the instances where psychosis and homosexuality are linked, the two are not essentially separate entities, but, as in all degrees of same-sex ambivalence, the two sides of one phenomenon. The 'psychosis' is the defensive barrier against the needed love-source, and the homosexuality is the resulting unmet love-need. Again, as in all degrees of same-sex ambivalence, either side may be latent or overt, or both, or neither. It is to be stressed that not all homosexuality is reinforced by a defensive barrier of this magnitude and severity, only the extreme end of the spectrum, that is all transsexuals but only some homosexuals. At the same time, it is also to be emphasised that this is not to condemn persons suffering from a marked degree of same-sex deficit. We would re-define psychosis as radically incomplete psychological growth, stemming from and at times still manifesting the psychological wounds of very early childhood. What we are speaking of is not 'craziness', but the suffering of little children.

Any incident that disrupts the child's attachment to the parent of the same sex may result in the homosexual condition, but it may be most clearly illustrated in the case of early separation.[2] Such separation, even if relatively brief, may lead to a typical process of mourning: protest at the absence of the loved parent, followed by despair, leading finally to detachment (Bowlby, 1973). When the child is reunited with the parent, it may take some time for normal attachment to be restored, since the child has experienced the parent as being hurtful ('he/she abandoned me') even if separation was unavoidable and there was no intention of hurt. The child may for a time show indifference, repressing his need for attachment, or alternate between hostility (detachment) and clinging behaviour (attachment). But what if the mourning process is never completely worked through? What if in some instances the child continues to repress his yearning for the love-source that has been experienced as hurtful and, at the same time, continues to repress his reproaches against the love-source, again on account of its hurtfulness and an unwillingness to trust the love source again? The resultant position would be an unmet love-need, consequent on and maintained by a defensive detachment from the needed love-source. This is precisely the kind of condition we have already spoken of, and here we would add to this by saying that this condition is essentially an unresolved pathological mourning process. Mourning as a psychological process can take place not only when a parent dies, but when the child is temporarily separated from the parent; or when parental behaviour hurts the child to such an extent that he or she represses the capacity for attachment to the parent. It is the absence of, and defence against, attachment to the parent that constitutes the psychological orphan.

Early absence of or separation from the parent of the same sex is often obvious in the case-histories of transsexuals (Walinder, 1967; Green, 1974; Stoller, 1975), though we have already said that the originating incident need not be immediately evident. The chief hypothesis to date about transsexualism (Stoller, 1975) has seen it as the result of a non-conflictual learning process, at least in the male-to-female transsexual. It is here suggested that transsexualism in both genders is based on conflict — on radical disidentification from the same sex, though this conflict may be very deeply repressed.

What we are speaking of is an intrapsychic wound, borne repressed within the personality since early childhood, which has checked a vital aspect of the normal process of psychological growth since that point of time. The unresolved 'mourning' process of a young child has persisted into adult years. As in any case of bereavement or hurt, the appropriate response is not hostility, fear, or bewilderment, but compassion. This should be true whatever the degree of same-sex deficit. Without such understanding and compassion, the actual intrinsic problem of homosexuality must perforce be needlessly intensified by society's unwillingness to comprehend and to care.

2
A NEW OUTLOOK

What does the homosexual question look like now, as a result of this re-evaluation? By focussing on the homosexual *condition* it becomes possible to reassess the nature of the problem and hence its solution. In this, it is important to focus on all aspects of the evidence, and to see the phenomenon of homosexuality as a whole — negative as well as positive, social as well as sexual — in order to ascertain what homosexuality is, and what it is not.

The homosexual condition is one of same-sex ambivalence, not just same-sex love. The love-need cannot be isolated from the defensive process that has shaped it and caused it to persist unmet. Unfortunately, the negative side of the ambivalence has often been ignored hitherto, or insufficiently taken into account. This lack of recognition for the negative side has led to an improper focussing on the positive side, and hence has resulted in partial and misleading definitions. The homosexual condition implies a problem in the capacity for relating to the same sex, and not merely a desire and facility for so doing. The checking of the same-sex identificatory process will mean that the homosexual is unable to relate in a truly heterosexual manner to the opposite sex. But the essential problem is one of incomplete same-sex psychological development, and it is vital that it should be recognised and dealt with as such.

In short, homosexuality is a phenomenon of same-sex ambivalence, not just same-sex love; and it is in itself a relational deficit vis-a-vis the same sex rather than vis-a-vis the opposite sex. These points are of major importance in stating what is and is not the problem of homosexuality.

What is problematical is the defensive detachment, and the missing growth consequent on this. However, the capacity for same-sex love is the attempt to restore this disrupted attachment and hence to make up for missing growth. It is not same-sex love needs that are pathological, but rather their lack of fulfilment. The capacity for same-sex love presupposes an underlying pathology (the defensive detachment), but is not itself pathological. Rather, it is quite the opposite — it is the attempt to resolve and heal the pathology. This does not imply that the solution should be acted out sexually, but it does imply that the solution should not be mistaken for the problem, as has often happened hitherto.

Attempted heterosexual relationships, or social contact with the opposite sex, are not the solution to homosexuality, since increased opposite-sex contact can do nothing to fulfil same-sex deficits. Relationships with the opposite sex are literally, by definition, irrelevant to a problem of this nature. Such a mistaken solution in fact leaves the problem untouched, or even confirms it. The capacity for same-sex love is the natural healing process, and it is most unfortunate that the bypassing or blocking of this process has often been mistaken for the solution. In this way much so-called healing of homosexuality has in fact been the direct opposite, since a wrong statement of the problem has in turn led to a wrong solution.

Both therapy and the task of ethical evaluation need to be based on adequate evidence. It has not been clear hitherto what homosexuality actually is, what precisely it is that we need to discuss and attempt to evaluate. One cannot make more than provisional judgements when one does not know what the condition is in itself. From the present evidence it would seem clear that the homosexual condition does not involve abnormal needs, but normal needs that have, abnormally, been left unmet in the ordinary process of growth. The needs as such are normal; their lack of fulfilment, and the barrier to their fulfilment, is abnormal. Just as the problem of homosexuality is twofold, there must likewise be a twofold therapeutic goal.

This twofold answer must be the undoing of the defensive detachment, and making up for unmet needs. Sexual activity may be an inappropriate solution. It is not, however, enough to discourage a mistaken solution without pointing to the proper solution, which is the meeting of same-sex needs without sexual activity. Hitherto, the Christian churches have tended to concentrate on preventing an improper response to the problem, and have failed to do much about getting started on the real answer.

At this point it may be asked why, if the homo-emotional drive is the solution to the problem, the problem is not often actually resolved in homosexual relationships. The first point to note is that such resolution can take place, and may well have done so more often than is known. Insufficient information is available here. There are, however, also certain obstacles to resolution. Firstly, both partners in a homosexual relationship have similar psychological needs, varying only in degree, and thus each partner's own needs and deficits render him or her less able to meet the other person's needs. Secondly, the deep dependency needs which are sometimes involved may not readily be met when the person concerned is chronologically an adult. Thirdly, and most significantly, the defensive detachment that was originally responsible for checking the normal process of growth may re-emerge and disrupt the renewed attachment. The instability of many homosexual relationships may well stem from this factor. The capacity for same-sex love is the solution to the problem of the homosexual condition, but unfortunately same-sex relationships face difficulties which may prevent their own fulfilment.

The fact that homo-emotional needs are often, though by no means always, eroticised, has tended to distract attention from the significance of the homosexual condition in itself. It is not surprising that someone who has attained physiological maturity should interpret his or her deepest emotional needs as sexual, but this is to mistake the essential character of these needs. Sexual expression is not appropriate to the normal parent-child relationship. Nor, as a corollary, is it appropriate to any relationship which, however adult in other respects, is significantly determined by the attempt to meet non-adult attachment needs. In the homosexual condition psychological needs that are essentially pre-adult remain in a person who is in other respects adult. Homosexual activity implies the eroticisation of deficits in growth that remain outstanding, and this is, fundamentally, a confusion of the emotional needs of the non-adult with the physiological desires of the adult. Sexuality is intended to express the desires both of physiological maturity and of psychological maturity, in co-ordination with each other. The one should not be isolated from the other. Where there is a lack of such co-ordination, deficits in growth should be fulfilled non-sexually, and in this way an integrated basis for a sexually expressed relationship will be attained.

An attachment to the same sex is not wrong, indeed it is precisely the right thing for meeting same-sex deficits. What is improper is the eroticisation of the friendship. Such eroticisation is secondary, and not essential to the homosexual condition as such. There are in any case many latent homosexuals who are not sufficiently aware of their emotional needs, and many non-practising homosexuals who choose not to act out such needs sexually whether or not the urge towards such eroticisation is strongly experienced. The term 'homosexuality' in fact begs the question. A non-sexual definition would be better, for although the condition may be, and often is, eroticised, it need not be. Such a term as 'homophilia' might be better, since it does not emphasise sexual activity. However, such a word would still focus undue attention on the need for same-sex love, while ignoring the underlying defensive detachment. The truest definition is neither homosexuality, nor homophilia, but same-sex ambivalence. It is this condition that exists prior to, and independently of, any sexual activity. Similarly, and most importantly, the needs involved can and should be met independently of sexual activity.

Arguing whether or not sexual acts are permissible for the homosexual is an important question, but, taken in isolation, it simply misses the main point. What is central is the underlying personality structure. And, since this condition is not essentially sexual, one should not set the homosexual question within the context of sexuality as a whole. To do so begs the question, and draws attention away from more important concerns. The question is not one of what is or is not acceptable in sexuality, since the question is not intrinsically sexual in the first place. The issue is one of what is necessary for growth and development to psychological maturity, and what one is to do to make up for deficits in this.

It has already been pointed out that marriage is a mistaken solution for homosexuality, since opposite-sex contact cannot remedy same-sex deficits. One may now also say that marriage is a mistaken point of comparison for homosexuality, since the essentially sexual and the essentially non-sexual may not rightly be regarded as analogous. On the evidence here presented, it should be clear that the true point of comparison for homosexuality is not sexual pair-bonding, but the parent-child relationship. It is vital to the whole task of evaluation that homosexuality should be set within this particular perspective.

The solution to the problem of the homosexual condition is not sexual activity. Unfortunately, mere abstinence from sexual activity has often been mistaken for the solution, without the realisation that there are certain legitimate psychological needs involved, which ought not to be left unmet. One should neither ignore unmet needs (the 'conservative' mistake), nor eroticise them (the 'liberal' mistake). It is the failure to understand this that has led to the polarisation of the debate on homosexuality.

Homosexuality involves both a state of incompletion and a drive towards completion. The normal process of psychological growth has been checked in a significant respect, but the potential for restoration is not absent, and the process of growth may be resumed. This reparative attempt is, we must repeat, the *solution* and not the *problem*. The normal process of growth has been interrupted and left unfulfilled, and the capacity for same-sex love is itself the attempt to restore the disrupted attachment. It is this that the homosexual strives towards.

Thus, the nature of the homosexual drive itself marks the fundamental criticism of the homosexual condition, and indicates that homosexuals are not satisfied with their state as it is. In other words it is the drive towards and longing for same-sex psychological completion that itself criticises the state of incompletion that it stems from and attempts to make good.

The end result of this process of growth is heterosexuality, understood as the capacity for relating to people as a psychologically complete member of one's own sex. It is not sexual activity with the opposite sex that defines the heterosexual, since such activity may be relatively superficial. The central criterion must be the nature and direction of the underlying psychological needs. True heterosexuality must be based on a heteropsychologic personality structure.

Heterosexuality, no less than homosexuality, has suffered from partial and misleading definitions hitherto. In particular, it has been a mistake to define heterosexuality solely vis-a-vis the opposite sex, and not as a state in itself. It implies the fulfilment of certain psychological needs, and not just a potential for sexual activity. There is the latter, but it is based on the former. Moreover, heterosexuality has definite implications for relating to the same sex as well as to the opposite sex. Relationships with the same sex are no longer governed by the need to fulfil an incomplete same-sex identity. Heterosexuality is the ability to relate to both sexes, not just to the opposite sex, as a psychologically complete member of one's own sex. It thus has social as well as sexual implications. Even vis-a-vis the opposite sex, many relationships will not be sexual, and yet the pattern of interaction will reflect the completion of the same-sex identificatory process.

Heterosexuality is in fact not just a matter of sexuality, but of gender identity, and of the fulfilment of psychological needs.

Much confusion has been caused by the consideration of relationships with the opposite sex in isolation from same-sex psychological fulfilment. It is not heterosexual behaviour as such that makes the heterosexual, but the fulfilment of same-sex needs. A heteropsychologic personality is based on the fulfilment of homosexual needs — the same legitimate psychological needs that are involved in the homosexual condition. Homosexuals relate to the same sex and the opposite sex as incomplete members of their own sex. The solution to this situation is for them to become complete members of their own sex. It is only thus that one becomes truly *heteros*, truly *other* (complementary) to the opposite sex.

Heterosexuality is the goal of human development, but it involves a heteropsychologic personality structure which is based on the fulfilment of homo-emotional needs and not on their checking. Indeed, unless and until same-sex needs are fulfilled, there can be no truly heteropsycholog-ical personality structure. Conversely, this implies that the fulfilment of homosexual needs would itself involve their abrogation. When deficits have been met, they have been met; and the attachment through which they have been met is rendered redundant. Homosexual relationships must therefore be regarded as inherently self-limiting, since they belong to the process of maturation, and cease if they have fulfilled their purpose. Homosexuality (same-sex incompletion) has a goal beyond itself, and that goal is heterosexuality (same-sex completion). By contrast, heterosexuality has no goal beyond itself. This is not to imply that all heterosexual relationships are stable and successful — many are not — but it is to state that there is nothing inherently self-limiting about heterosexuality. Heterosexuals may have a variety of emotional problems or immaturities, but heterosexuality as such is never 'cured', because it is not something requiring to be healed in the first place.

Since homosexuality is marked by incompletion, that is by the absence of some degree of normal growth, the homosexual cannot act as if growth has been completed. The bisexual may have a lesser degree of same-sex deficit, but otherwise the psychodynamic structure here is the same as in other degrees of homosexuality. In any case, it is improper to speak of homosexuality as a fear of, or flight from, heterosexuality. Heterosexuality has not yet been attained, in greater or lesser degree. And one may not properly be said to renounce what one has not yet attained.

In this way it may be seen how the traditional label of 'immaturity', so often applied to homosexuality, has in fact a twofold implication. Immaturity, or rather, incomplete growth, does imply that the homosexual condition is not normative. It is not the goal of human development. But to assert this by itself is insufficient. One must also assert that the psychological needs involved are a normal and essential part of the process of human growth, and that they cannot be bypassed without the goal itself being rendered permanently unattainable. To reiterate, we are speaking of normal and universal psychological needs, the needs that are usually met through the growing child's attachment to the parent of the same sex. What is abnormal is that these needs should be left unmet; what is normal is that they should be met. And in most people these needs have been met. In evaluating the homosexual condition, it would be helpful to bear this point in mind. In this specialised technical sense, every adult heterosexual is an 'ex – homosexual'. This does not imply that adult heterosexuals have necessarily had previous experience of homosexual activity (though some have). What it does imply is that the adult heterosexual has been able to relate adequately to the parent of the same sex during the process of growth, and that same – sex attachment needs have thus been fulfilled.

What is abnormal about the homosexual condition is that the needs involved have been left unmet. The needs as such are normal, and should be met. This is what is implied by the phrase 'becoming heterosexual': the fulfilment of same-sex attachment needs, and hence the fulfilment, and not the checking, of the homosexual's own deepest emotional longings.

Perhaps paradoxically, it is homosexual love that is itself the striving for heterosexuality, understood as same-sex psychological completeness. The homosexual may not consciously seek heterosexuality, or may even claim that he has no wish to seek it. This is due to not realising the significance of the homosexual urge, and to mistaken ideas about what it means to become heterosexual. Yet it is the fulfilment of homosexual needs that *is* the capacity for heterosexual response. And this is really tautologous: becoming a psychologically complete member of one's own sex (i.e. the fulfilment of homosexual needs) enables one to relate to others as a psychologically complete member of one's own sex (i.e. the ability to relate as a heterosexual). The homosexual is potentially heterosexual on this basis, and only on this basis. Unless and until homosexual needs have been met there is no basis for a truly heterosexual response.

The suppression of the homosexual response is not to be equated with the elimination of the needs involved in homosexuality. A non-practising homosexual is still a homosexual, in whom there are certain deficits and unmet needs. For this reason the suppression of homosexual acts cannot be equated with healing. Eroticisation may be unacceptable, but the problem of deficits in growth remains, and it is only the meeting of these needs that may justifiably be regarded as healing. To block the fulfilment of homosexual needs is to block the restoration of the normal process of growth. Or, in other words, to block the fulfilment of such needs is to block the very path towards mature heterosexuality, and to confirm the individual in an essentially pre-heterosexual position. Such a manoeuvre is certainly no solution, but merely a confirmation of the problem. To disrupt or suppress the homosexual's reparative drive only ensures that the problem of the homosexual condition *cannot* be resolved.

The capacity for same-sex love is itself the natural healing process for a state of same-sex deficits, and it is vital that one should cooperate with this process and not check it. The persistence of the defensive detachment implies that homosexual relationships face inherent difficulties which may prevent their own fulfilment. And therapists, whether secular or Christian, may try to block such fulfilment in the name of 'cure'. It is nothing less than tragic that the solution to a problem should be mistaken for the actual problem. It is only a true understanding of the problem that can lead to its true solution. Healing for the homosexual is entirely possible — but it has not yet genuinely been tried!

3
THE CHRISTIAN POSITION REASSESSED

Traditionally, the Christian faith has regarded homosexual activity as inappropriate, as contrary to the will and
purposes of God for mankind. The scriptural evidence has
been reiterated by subsequent Christian pronouncements,
and it is only in contemporary debate that this position
has been seriously questioned. The details of this debate
have been adequately covered elsewhere.[1]. It is not
proposed to discuss this here, but to suggest a fresh
perspective on the debate. The scriptural references to
homosexuality are: Genesis 19:1-11; Leviticus 18:22,
20:13; Judges 19:22-25; Romans 1:26,27; I Corinthians
6:9; I Timothy 1:9-11. However much one may wish, quite
legitimately, to qualify or contextualise these references, it
seems to the present writer that one may not avoid the
conclusion that homosexual acts are always condemned
and never approved. The need for reassessment is not to
be found at this point. However, the traditional view may
properly and significantly be reassessed in another way.
The whole thrust of this study has been that it is mistaken
to concentrate primarily on homosexual acts, as these are
secondary and not essential to the homosexual condition.
To evaluate the latter — as a state of psychological
incompletion and a corresponding striving for completion
— one should turn, not to guidelines for adult sexuality,
but to considerations of pre-adult development, in
particular to the parent-child relationship. Neglect of this
has been the glaring weakness of the traditional Christian
viewpoint.

In Genesis 1:27 it is stated that God created us male and
female, 'in his own image'. This is frequently repeated in
traditional statements about homosexuality. Kent

Philpott says: 'Homosexuality needs to be presented as it relates to God's creating man male and female.' [2] Michael Green notes that God's image 'is displayed ... not in man with man or woman with woman, but in man and woman in community'[3] and that 'it is in the complementarity of the man-woman relationship that we see his will for our species'.[4] Likewise, David Watson: 'Biologically we are either male or female ... and it is together, male and female, that we exhibit the image of God'.[5] These are fundamental points, which certainly need to be affirmed. However, great care must be taken in applying them to homosexuality. The complementarity of male and female is certainly in God's plan, but it is in God's plan for adulthood. Men and women are not born adult. Rather, we are designed to undergo a long period of physiological and psychological development before reaching maturity. Men and women *are* complementary — as adults. Children are in the process of attaining the mature identity that implies complementarity. But neither children, nor persons in whom the normal developmental process is checked, have yet reached such complementarity. It is true that 'no-one is born a homosexual'[6] but no-one is born a heterosexual either, and it is vital that we should do justice to the significance of pre-adult development in God's plan.

The complementarity argument must not be used in such a way as to imply bypassing the need for growth and development. Michael Green says that homosexuality, along with adultery, bestiality and fornication, 'violate God's intention, that man and woman should constitute one flesh in which his image is reflected'.[7] This comparison is not exact. Sexual sin is contrary to God's intention, but homosexuality, although often an occasion for sexual sin, is essentially a state of incomplete development. It is the incompletion that is contrary to God's intention here. Homosexual acts are prohibited, not because they repudiate the man-woman relationship,[8] but because sexual expression is not appropriate to pre-adult relationships.

In this sense it is misleading to say that 'homosexuality

is wrong because it frustrates that complementarity between male and female in which the divine image is to be seen'.[9] Homosexuality is not a matter of 'symbolic dissonance'.[10] The homosexual condition does not militate against male-female complementarity, but rather provides a paradoxical confirmation of such complementarity by confirming the need for the normal means of attaining such complementarity. It is incorrect to speak of homosexual expression as 'endangering the formation of sexual identity in boys and girls'.[11] Sexual activity may be inappropriate, but the same-sex love-urge is itself the attempt to make good deficits in sexual identity. It is the attainment of male-female complementarity that is God's plan — but this is the goal of human development, not something given 'ready-made' right from the start.

The scriptural understanding of sexuality as a whole is often taken to be the proper context for the discussion of homosexuality. This may be misleading if sexuality is equated with sexual activity, since, as we have seen, homosexuality is not essentially a sexual condition. In this respect, the scriptures may only provide negative guidelines: the eroticisation of the homosexual condition is prohibited, but this is only one side of the matter. If sexuality is understood more broadly, in terms of gender identity and not just sexual activity, the homosexual condition may well be seen against the background of male-female complementarity, in the way that has just been suggested. We may affirm, with David Holloway, that 'God intended one heterosexual humanity'.[12] We may also affirm that the division into 'two types of humanity, one heterosexual and the other homosexual, is to be seen as fallen'.[13] But what is 'fallen' here is the fact that some people have a complete same-sex identity (heterosexuality) while others have an incomplete same-sex identity (homosexuality). The goal is the attainment of a complete same-sex identity; and, where the process of growth has been checked, the reparative drive of same-sex love is the solution to the problem of underlying deficits.

The reparative striving is the solution and not the

problem. This point must be of central importance for the ethical debate. And the implications of this point are twofold. Firstly, the fact that same-sex love is itself the striving for psychological completion implies that it is mistaken for homosexuals to assume that God intended them to be as they are, that is, incomplete. It begs the question to say that 'God must have deliberately designed them that way'.[14] The homosexual condition *as it is* is not 'in the image of God' as is sometimes suggested by homosexuals. God did not create homosexuals *as* homosexuals, but as men and women who are intended to attain psychological maturity in their gender identity. The 'image' argument must be correctly interpreted. The mistake of some heterosexuals is to overlook the fact that growth is required towards this goal, and that one may not expect to see the goal until the process of growth is completed. The mistake of some homosexuals is to assume that the goal has already been reached, when in fact development has been checked and still requires completion. It is precisely because God has designed man and woman to be 'in his image' that he wishes to deal with all that falls short of this, and to fulfil the normal process of growth. Through the fulfilment of same-sex needs, homosexuals are in the process of becoming what God intends for them. Norman Pittenger, in his plea for the legitimacy of homosexual expression, uses the phrase 'in process' in a broader, nonspecific sense. Referring to people in general and not just homosexuals, he says:

The important thing is that the person shall be *on the way, moving towards* the goal and *open to* the possibilities which conspire to promote such actualization. He is not *yet* fulfilled; he is *being* fulfilled. Man, like the rest of creation, is 'in process' towards the greatest good; he has not yet arrived there.[15]

It is perhaps ironical that a study of homosexuality based on 'process theology' has not grasped the special sense in which homosexuals, as homosexuals, may truly be said to be 'in process' — striving for the psychological completion of gender identity that has not yet been attained.

The second implication of the reparative striving is that healing must imply the fulfilment of unmet needs. God does not cure people of legitimate needs. To block the homosexual urge, as distinct from its sexual expression, is to block the very process of healing. In this sense, it is quite improper to speak of homosexuals as 'individuals trapped by forces beyond their control',[16] or as 'in bondage to their habit'.[17] It is not a matter of bondage to be subject to normal and legitimate developmental needs, and it is only the fulfilment of such needs that may justifiably be regarded as healing. Similarly, it may be misleading to speak of deliverance from homosexual temptation. Deliverance from the sexual expression of homosexual needs is right and proper. But it must be clear that such deliverance applies to inappropriate means of meeting such needs, not to the needs themselves. Otherwise, to speak of deliverance from homosexual temptation is tantamount to saying that a child should be 'delivered' from its normal love-need for the parent of the same sex!

In parenthesis, one may add that it is not plausible that Jesus Christ in his incarnate life experienced homosexual temptation, as some Christian writers have suggested.[18] The homosexual urge arises where there has been a deficit in the relationship with the parent of the same sex. However, the scriptures testify to Jesus' close and deep communion with his heavenly Father — a relationship such that there could be no possible basis for speaking of a deficit and a drive to make good this deficit, i.e. the homosexual urge.

A homosexual who no longer engages in sexual activity may be spoken of as an 'ex-practising homosexual', but no-one is an 'ex-homosexual' unless and until unmet same-sex needs have been fulfilled. The goal is not change as such, but fulfilment — a fulfilment that would in turn imply change. It may be said that God 'does not always choose to change the orientation of a Christian homosexual'.[19] One may venture to suggest that this limitation is more ours than God's. Until healing is seen to involve the fulfilment of homosexual needs, and not their checking, we shall constantly be hindering rather than cooperating with God's purposes for the homosexual.

The importance of such cooperation cannot be underestimated. John White notes that 'man's personality develops and changes for better or worse in accordance with divine laws. Those who study those laws ... can give real help by using them'.[20] More specifically, Richard Lovelace states:

> Just because gender identity is not wholly biologically determined does not mean that it is not God's creative intent that we work to shape sexual identity so that those who are biologically masculine reach full psychological masculinity also, and channel their sexual responses toward women.[21]

It is vital that the affirmation of divine laws for development should be correctly interpreted. The attainment of same-sex psychological completion implies the fulfilment of same-sex psychological needs — needs that may not be bypassed if the goal is to be attained. Same-sex needs are to be fulfilled, for this is in accordance with the God-given laws for human development, before, and as a condition of, relating to the opposite sex as heterosexual.

Legitimate needs are to be met in legitimate ways, that is to say, non-sexually. The Bible 'does not veto same-sex friendships',[22] and 'deep friendships ... must be as right for homosexuals as for heterosexuals'.[23] Such friendships are central, and indeed essential, to the solution of the problem of homosexuality.

In the light of this analysis, it is proper not to make blanket statements about homosexuality. Numerous Christian writers have in practice blurred the all-important distinction between the homosexual condition and homosexual acts. David Holloway states: 'he is not a God whose intention is homosexuality'.[24] This kind of point is made even more forcibly by Kent Philpott:

> Homosexuality is ... the most extreme form rebellion can take because it is acting in exact opposition to the way God created us ... We see no hint of

homosexuality in the accounts of the creation at all. So then, when God prohibits homosexuality He preserves the natural order of the creation. Homosexuality is unnatural, it is against the creation of God ... A true homosexual has accepted something that is totally contrary to reality.[25]

Such statements are both true and false. They are true in asserting the impropriety of homosexual activity, which is the eroticisation of pre-adult psychological needs. But they are incorrect and utterly misleading if taken to imply that no legitimate needs are involved in the homosexual condition. The homosexual urge as such is entirely in accordance with the will of God and the divine intention in creation. It is neither unrealistic nor rebellious, since it belongs to the maturational process that is the will of God for human development. To condemn homosexual love, as distinct from its eroticisation, is to condemn the child's love-need for his or her parent. The needs are normal; the fact that they have been left unmet in the process of growth is abnormal. Thus, it is the deficits that are against the will of God, and not the attempt to meet them. God did not intend the normal maturational process to be checked. But he did intend persons to attain adulthood through a parental attachment, and did intend that the maturational process should be resumed if interrupted. In this sense, we may agree with Norman Pittenger that it is 'absurd' to regard the homosexual's desires as 'the very contradiction of genuine humanity'.[26] The desires in themselves, prior to eroticisation, are normal and necessary to human development. Similarly, provided that one distinguishes the desires from their eroticisation, one may also affirm that 'when homosexual men and women try to live "in love" ... they are fulfilling themselves and acting in accordance with God's purpose'.[27]

God *did* intend the parent-child relationship, and that is essentially what we are talking about, for the homosexual condition implies that non-adult psychological needs remain in a person who may in other respects be adult. The parent-child relationship is not illicit; it is in God's plan. It is misleading to say, without qualification, that 'it is not a man who will fulfil man's desire for community, but someone who is distinctly "other" '.[28] Such a statement is true only of psychological maturity, and not of the pre-adult state. A man does, properly, fulfil a man's desire for community in the father-son relationship. And a woman does, properly, fulfil a woman's desire for community in the mother-daughter relationship. Relationships such as these are within the purposes of God, and their significance must not be overlooked.

It is sometimes suggested that homosexuality under-mines the family: 'to affirm the homosexual way as an alternative ... is to do something radical to the social consciousness as it affects the family'.[29] This again misunderstands the significance of homosexuality, and indeed implies a one-dimensional view of the family, by focussing on the adult relationship of the man and woman, and not taking parent-child relationships into account. Homosexuality is not 'anti-family', but rather it is a paradoxical confirmation of the need for the family and of the importance of the child being able to receive parental care. In attempting to make good certain deficits in the parent-child relationship, homosexuality implicitly affirms the importance of the needs that it is trying to fulfil.

As a corollary to this, it may be noted that to ask a homosexual not to meet his needs at all, as distinct from meeting them improperly, is like forcing a child to make do without a parent or parent-substitute. In this way the lack of fulfilment of normal family life can only be perpetuated, and the persistence of psychological deficits may be detrimental to the person concerned. The homosexual has a greater need for relationships than a single heterosexual, because the former involves a child's need for his parent rather than the need of one adult for another. To be a single adult is one thing; to be a parentless child is quite another matter.

Precisely in affirming the family, the Bible affirms the propriety of same-sex love, understood as the love-need of a child for his or her parent. When deficits occur, substitute relationships for parental care are in God's redemptive plan, just as parental relationships are in his creative plan. A notable scriptural theme is that of the care of orphans. The scriptural understanding of homosexuality is not exhausted by consideration of specific references to homosexual activity, or to more general discussion of human sexuality. This is only one side of the evidence, and the negative side at that as far as homosexuality is concerned. In order to consider the scriptural evidence as a whole, which is important, one must look for passages relating to the significance of the homosexual condition, even though this may be referred to implicitly rather than explicitly. Positive guidelines *are* provided (not just negative ones, as is commonly assumed), and these guidelines are to be found in the concern for making good deficits in parental care, i.e. in caring for orphans.

The duty of care for orphans and the denunciation of their oppression is a theme to be found throughout the Old Testament. Ill-treatment of the orphan is condemned, as in Isaiah 1:23, Jeremiah 5:28 and Ezekiel 22:7. There is a reiterated prohibition of such oppression:

You shall not ill-treat any ... fatherless child (Exodus 22:22). You shall not deprive ... orphans of justice (Deuteronomy 24:17). A curse upon him who withholds justice from ... the orphan (Deuteronomy 27:19). Do not ill-treat or do violence to ... the orphan (Jeremiah 22:3). Do not oppress the orphan (Zechariah 7:10).

One is enjoined to give the orphan his rights (Isaiah 1:17), and in the New Testament such help is seen as essential to acceptable religion (James 1:27). Above all, this concern is linked with the character of God himself. It is God who protects and helps orphans (Deuteronomy 10:18, Psalms 10:18, 146:9), for he is himself the 'father of the fatherless' (Psalm 68:5). 'In thee the fatherless find a father's love' (Hosea 14:3).

The perfect will of God for human growth is checked whenever a child is orphaned. However, although being an orphan is in this sense 'against the will of God', one does not therefore seek to punish an orphan for being an orphan. Rather, to seek the will of God in such a situation implies doing all that one can to make good whatever deficits are involved. By analogy, the homosexual condition, as involving deficits in the ability to relate to the parent of the same sex, is not culpable as such, but rather requires the resolution of the deficits in question. To thwart the resolution of these deficits and to hinder the fulfilment of unmet needs is comparable to oppressing the orphan, indeed is a form of such oppression. To facilitate the needed fulfilment is as acceptable as are other forms of helping orphans.

Unmet needs are to be met — but without eroticisation. It is the sexual expression of pre-adult psychological needs that is unacceptable, and it is in this sense that one may say that God did not intend homosexuality. The needs are legitimate: the only question is of the legitimate means of fulfilling such needs when they have not been met in the ordinary process of growth.

The homosexual condition may not be evaluated within the context of human sexuality as a whole. It is not enough to assert that the Bible restricts sexual activity to heterosexual marriage,[30] or that this is 'a complete picture of sexuality as God ordained it'.[31] Such statements may be true, but they are beside the point. That point is the propriety and fulfilment of non-sexual relationships in the process of maturation. We are not questioning 'God's plan for sexuality'.[32] Indeed, one may wholeheartedly affirm that 'no Church which claims the name of Christian is at liberty to repudiate something which is central to creation and redemption'.[33] This is not however, relevant to the central issue of same-sex psychological deficits. One is not questioning the biblical guidelines for sexuality by pointing out that the question under consideration is not essentially sexual. The nub of the matter is that sexuality is the wrong area of comparison. The parent-child relationship, and the facilitating of human maturation, is the correct comparison.

Love is important, but not all love is intended to be

sexual. Indeed, even for the heterosexual only the marital relationship is intended to be sexual. All other relationships — with relatives, friends, and colleagues — are meant to be non-sexual. Love is far wider than its manifestation in sexual expression. For this reason one may not agree with Norman Pittenger that 'the way in which we come to know love and to exist in love is based upon, or grounded in, our having a sexual nature'[34]. One may readily agree when Pittenger speaks of 'the goodness of human sexuality'[35] and declares that 'all the negatives presuppose the positive goodness of sexuality itself'.[36] We are not questioning the goodness of human sexuality, but simply stating that 'homosexuality' — misleadingly so-called — is not essentially a sexual condition.

The Christian ideal of permanence in sexual relationships indicates a reason for the inappropriateness of homosexual activity. Homosexual relationships may last for only a brief length of time, or they may last for many years. However, if same-sex ambivalence were resolved and unmet needs fulfilled, the relationship would be outgrown, just as children normally outgrow their relationship of dependence on their parents. The difficulties in the way of such resolution and fulfilment have already been outlined. The point here is that the nature of the homosexual reparative drive is such as to make homosexual relationships inherently self-limiting. There is no basis for permanence in the structure of the homosexual condition. Mere duration indicates only the continuing lack of resolution of same-sex deficits, or else the fact that much time is needed to make good substantial deficits. A form of marriage to sanction the homosexual relationship would be inappropriate, because the relationship is inherently self-limiting, and because marriage is not right for a relationship analogous to that between parent and child. Marriage is a heterosexual 'institution'. As the homosexual reparative drive is itself a striving for the same-sex psychological completeness that is heterosexuality, homosexuality cannot be considered on a par with heterosexuality.

Both homosexual and heterosexual acts are inappropriate for the homosexual. To say that sexual activity is for heterosexual marriage is to assert that it is appropriate for the heteropsychologic personality, for the person who has attained same-sex psychological completion, and who is not in this respect still in the process of psychological growth. Marriage cannot be a cure for homosexuality, since a relationship with the opposite sex cannot deal with same-sex deficits. Indeed, the practice of heterosexuality may bring unhappiness not only to the homosexual but to the heterosexual partner.[37] This is not to deny that some married homosexuals may in greater or lesser degree have a satisfactory relationship with their partner, but the difficulties in such a relationship should not be lost sight of.

The legitimacy of homosexual needs must be central to the statement of the nature of the homosexual problem and its solution. Christian writers, no less than secular writers, have tended to be content with partial and misleading definitions. Attraction for the same sex is not in fact an adequate definition in itself.[38] Such attraction constitutes only one side of the same-sex ambivalence that is the homosexual condition. And ignorance of the overall phenomenon has resulted in the reparative drive being seen as the problem, rather than the solution to the underlying problem. Homosexuality is a same-sex relational deficit, not an opposite-sex one. Thus, it is incorrect to say that 'a homosexual's urge in one direction is blocked'[39] when referring to the opposite sex; or that a dam has been built 'against normal feelings of interest in the other sex'.[40] The barrier in the homosexual is the defensive detachment vis-a-vis the same sex. Only the resolution of this barrier, and the fulfilment of unmet same-sex needs, may justifiably be regarded as the answer to the homosexual question. Homosexual acts are not essential to the homosexual condition, and to define homosexuality in terms of its secondary eroticisation must be seen as utterly misleading.[41] Thus, too, abstinence as such is not the solution, but merely the prevention of an inappropriate acting-out of the solution. In principle, the abstinence required of the homosexual should be only temporary, pending the resolution and fulfilment of same-sex deficits. If same-sex needs were to be fully and truly met the erstwhile homosexual would have attained the psychological basis for sexual fulfilment in a heterosexual relationship.

From this reassessment of the traditional distinction between the homosexual condition and homosexual acts, it may be seen how the current polarisation of the homosexual debate is ultimately a false dichotomy. Only insufficient understanding of the concerns of each side leads to divergence. If fulfilment is seen as merely sexual, or if healing is seen as merely the suppression of sexual activity, both of these approaches miss the heart of the matter. There *are* legitimate needs involved in the homosexual condition. These ought not to be met sexually, but they ought to be met. This is the main point at stake.

HEALING AND PRAYER

To 'stop being a homosexual' means to stop being a person with same-sex psychological deficits. This can only happen through the fulfilment of such needs and the resolution of any barriers to such fulfilment. Conversely, it must be understood very clearly that to thwart the fulfilment of such needs implies that the person is forced to remain homosexual. A non-practising homosexual is still a homosexual. Sexual activity may not be appropriate to the outworking of the solution, but sexual abstinence of itself does not begin to meet the problem of the underlying deficits. Only the nonsexual fulfilment of same-sex needs may do this.

The homosexual cannot just 'turn heterosexual', bypassing the normal route to heterosexuality. The goal of development may not be attained without passing through the process towards the goal. Same-sex needs are to be fulfilled — according to the natural, God-given laws for human growth — before relating to the opposite sex as heterosexual. Much advice to homosexuals has, by implication, tried to bypass this process of growth. The healing process of growth is to be promoted, and not blocked, short-circuited or bypassed. Thus, it is important not to pray about heterosexuality directly, but about the fulfilling of homosexual needs, which, if truly accomplished, will lead to heterosexuality, and without which heterosexuality cannot be truly attained.

It is often difficult for a homosexual to change. This difficulty is to a large extent based on our incorrect ideas about what such change would involve. It must be stressed that the homosexual really seeks to fulfil legitimate needs, and that it would be 'contrary to nature' to expect to bypass these needs or leave them unfulfilled. However, if such needs were truly fulfilled, the homosexual would be changed.

One should not try to cure, or ask God to cure, something for which cure is not necessary. God does not 'cure' people of legitimate needs. Rather, the Christian faith indicates the proper, as distinct from inappropriate, means of fulfilling such needs. It is not merely ironic, but tragic, that people have attempted to 'cure' what should rightly be fulfilled. Ministries to homosexuals have not yet realised the significance of these legitimate needs. It is sometimes assumed that conversion will 'cure' homosexuality, and this has led to distress when homosexual desires persist or return after conversion. However, since such desires are based on legitimate needs, it is hardly surprising that the desires will persist so long as the needs remain unmet. No-one is an ex-homosexual, as distinct from an ex-practising homosexual, unless and until homosexual needs have been met. God can and does overrule prayer, but it helps if we cooperate with the healing process, rather than block it. It is we who have limited the scope of what God seeks to do.

There is a great need for both the churches and society in general to be more open to homosexuals. Homophobia, or any degree of reluctance and antipathy, is unjustified, and blocks healing just as effectively as inappropriate therapeutic measures. The homosexual condition, as distinct from homosexual activity, is not reprehensible. By way of corollary, various Christian writers, while clearly opposing homosexual activity, have equally clearly declared that it is appropriate to ordain non-practising homosexuals.[1]

The possibility of healing — a healing that is essentially a fulfilment — is meant to be actualised. In Christian ministry, as in conventional therapy, the goal should be twofold: the defensive detachment vis-a-vis the same sex is to be undone, and unmet needs are to be met, to make up for the missing growth consequent on the defensive barrier. Relationships and prayer may serve as the means towards this twofold goal. Relationships will be considered first, though for the Christian these should not be separate from prayer, but supported by it and serving as a practical outworking of prayer.

Relational deficits imply the need for corrective interpersonal experience. Homosexuality is the kind of problem that needs to be solved through relationships. The solution to same-sex deficits is to be sought through the medium of one or more non-sexual relationships with members of the same sex (members of the same anatomic sex, in the case of transsexuals). The supportive and healing relationship must be gender-specific, because of the very nature of the problem. The male homosexual needs a male helper, and the female homosexual a female helper. A relationship between a heterosexual and a homosexual of the same sex is likely to be more stable than that beween two homosexuals, and it is important that more heterosexuals as well as homosexuals become involved in this ministry. It is the provision of good same-sex relationships that helps to meet unmet same-sex needs, heal defects in the relational capacity, and in this way forward the healing process. Psychological growth is normally mediated through relationships, and 'reparative growth' — the process of making up for missing growth — may be expected to take place in similar manner. The same-sex attachment is itself therapeutic, and both sides of the twofold therapeutic process may be worked out within the context of such a relationship. The homosexual is not to stop loving members of the same sex, but to meet his or her psychological needs deeply and completely without sexual activity. The same-sex relationship is to be so fulfilling that same-sex deficits remain no longer and the relationship itself is outgrown. It may be difficult at first for some Christians to accept that same-sex needs should be fulfilled, but this is necessary and it does not imply sexual activity. One will do well to remember that the capacity for same-sex love is essentially the love-need of the child for the parent, even if not consciously experienced as such. The homo-emotional drive thus seeks the fulfilment of this aspect of family life, and it is right and good that Christians should help towards this fulfilment. To do this is, in a special sense, to offer a home to the homeless (Isaiah 58:7), as God himself is said to do (Psalm 68:6).

Prayer for psychological healing will be of great importance towards the fulfilment of God's purposes for the homosexual, as indeed it is for other persons. Prayer is at the heart of healing, and God's love is concerned with all aspects of the brokenness of our lives. We can offer him all of our past as well as our present and our future. This does not mean writing off the past, but opening it up to the healing love of Christ. The undoing and transformation of the effects of the past is one of our greatest needs. Since so many of these effects consist of things we are not fully aware of, we should offer God our unconscious as well as our conscious life. It is our whole personality, and not just one level of it, that is to be redeemed and healed. Francis MacNutt affirms that 'Jesus, as Lord of time, is able to do what we cannot: he can heal those wounds of the past that still cause us suffering'.[2] Ruth Carter Stapleton speaks similarly of our subconscious memory: 'The only means we have of revising this emotional record is by the re-creative work of the Holy Spirit. And often the Spirit must redo our earliest recollections.'[3] Likewise, Reginald East: 'As the Holy Spirit brings the painful to consciousness, we can help them to let Christ Jesus enter into it and act to heal.'[4]

It is God who heals, and so our dependency on God is all-important. Listening is vital to the ministry of healing, and it should be twofold: listening to the other person, and listening to God, in a continuing and deepening sensitivity to the guidance of the Holy Spirit. It is the Holy Spirit who will bring to awareness points of stress and pain, whatever it is within the life of a person that requires prayerful attention. Our part is to pray, and to allow God to work as he will.

As regards homosexuals, one is to cooperate with the

natural healing process, and to deal with whatever hinders
the fulfilment of this reparative drive. The negative side of
same-sex ambivalence requires particular attention — all
the more so as this negative aspect has not generally been
recognised as part of the homosexual condition. The
defensive detachment vis-a-vis members of the same sex
originated when the child experienced the parent of the
same sex as hurtful (whether intentionally or involuntari-
ly hurtful); and the hurt was such that the child repressed
its normal need for attachment to that parent (even if at a
conscious level there might appear to be little difficulty in
the relationship). The defensive detachment marks an
inability to trust the needed love-source, a 'decision' not to
receive love from that love-source any longer. The
'decision' is, however, beyond conscious and voluntary
control. It is a pre-adult decision, and in some cases may
even date from the very earliest years. It cannot be
reversed merely by a conscious effort of will-power, but
requires healing.

Whether or not the parent was culpable, the child
experienced animosity towards the parent, and so a deep
forgiveness is important. Such forgiveness acts as spiritual
surgery for the person who forgives, acting on the
persisting animosity. Moreover, if the parent was
culpable, such forgiveness also becomes significant for the
person forgiven. The sense of hurt and resentment may to
a greater or lesser degree be unconscious, and so the need
for forgiveness may become more apparent as the healing
process brings to light the hurts of the past. Forgiveness is
often difficult, and a basic prayer may be for the ability to
forgive. Further possible steps may be to ask God's
forgiveness for one's own lack of forgiveness; to ask God
to change one's desire to cling to resentment so as to
become more truly willing to forgive; and to pray
positively for the wellbeing of the person to be forgiven,
remembering that this person too is beloved by God.
Where one's own forgiveness falls short, one may ask the
indwelling Christ to forgive in and through oneself, to
enable one to forgive not in one's own strength, but

through the power of the Holy Spirit.

Forgiveness may be linked with the healing of the actual relationship with the parent, or of the memories of that relationship. However, the homosexual condition implies that the negativity towards the same-sex parent has been transferred to members of the same sex in general. It is the homosexual's general relational capacity that must be dealt with, and the transference of attitudes originating vis-a-vis the parent may be worked through in any current relationship with a member of the same sex.

Negative responses to early hurt have persisted unresolved, and in connection with this there will be a particular need for the healing of memories. Since the defensive detachment is essentially an unresolved 'mourning' process (see Chapter I) such 'mourning' must be worked through. Within the subconscious mind there may be anger and a concomitant sense of grievance at the apparent or intentional hurtfulness of the parent. There will also be a sense of loss as the attachment to the parent is disrupted, and indeed an abiding sense of loss as the need for attachment is repressed and the normal process of growth-through-attachment is checked. There may, specifically, be a sense of rejection due to the loss of attachment, or actual depression, or a sense of inferiority. Loss also implies loneliness, again resulting from the absence of the normal and necessary attachment. And if the repression of the need for attachment took place very early, an overwhelming fear and anguish may be brought to light. To the very young child, the parent is his or her source of being, and so one's very being is felt to be endangered if the attachment to the parent is disrupted. In other instances, the anguish at loss may not be so great. In all instances, however, there is hurt; and frequently much of the hurt will not be conscious, or else conscious expressions of same-sex negativity will not be recognised for what they are — the persistence of early hurts experienced in the parent-child relationship.

There is a deep inability to trust, which in origin was the unwillingness to trust again in a love-source which was experienced as hurtful. It is this lack of trust which is central to the repression of the need for attachment. Trust involves openness to the love-source: it involves attachment rather than detachment. Attachment to the love-source implies the ability to receive love; detachment implies an inability to receive love, and hence the absence of the psychological growth that normally takes place through receiving love.

It is not strictly necessary to find out when the defensive detachment took place, or how it was caused. The actual or probable cause may at times be obvious or else become apparent in the course of healing. However, since the hurts of the past and the need to make up for missing growth have persisted into the present, the past is effective and accessible in the present, and may be dealt with as a relational deficit in the present. Here and now, the wounded child of previous years may be made whole, as the residues of the past are transferred to and reactivated in the present. The ability to remember may often facilitate the healing process, but the repetition within present relationships of the pattern of past relationships is itself an acted-out form of memory, which makes the past available in the present.

Every aspect of the wounds of the past may be held to the love of Jesus Christ for his healing. However, inner healing is more than just the healing of memories or of emotions attached to those memories. This is only one side of the matter, and there are also the consequences of past hurts to be dealt with. The defensive detachment blocks the fulfilling of legitimate same-sex needs, and it is not enough just to undo the defensive detachment. Unmet needs must still be met in order to make up for missing growth. It must always be remembered that the therapeutic task is in this way twofold. In practice, the fulfilment of unmet needs will almost certainly require the outworking of supportive same-sex relationships as well as prayer, particularly where the deficit involved is very extensive. Relationships are the normal medium for psychological growth within the purposes of God. As such, it is important to make the fullest possible use of them, as God-given channels for healing. For the homosexual this will involve the fulfilment of needs that would ordinarily have been met through the attachment to the parent of the same sex. These can and should be fulfilled without sexual activity. But they will not be fulfilled unless there are people who are willing to provide good non-sexual relationships. The churches cannot seek healing for the homosexual at a distance, since this is effectively a contradiction in terms. There must be a more widespread involvement.

The fulfilment of unmet needs will require the time and active concern of a continuing relationship. It may be said that 'the conclusion of a prayer for inner healing usually involves a filling with God's love of all the empty places in our hearts'.[5] The fulfilment of this prayer will in many instances be mediated through human channels, as prayer and relationships normally complement each other to forward the process of psychological healing. At the heart of it all, Christ himself is the healer. A prayer particularly recommended by Ruth Carter Stapleton is that Jesus will be the bridge between the love you knew in your early years and the love you should have known.[6] For the homosexual this prayer will specifically ask Jesus to bridge the gap vis-a-vis the parent of the same sex, to make up for the love that the homosexual was unable to receive as a result of repressing the need for attachment. Whether or not love was subsequently offered to the child, it was not received by him or her, and it is this inability to receive love in the ordinary process of growth that is the poignant crux of the homosexual condition.

A particularly sympathetic discussion of homosexuality is to be found in the works of Ruth Carter Stapleton. However, one may venture to suggest that her discussion does not yet cover the full scope of the problem. The strength of her presentation lies in its recognition of the homosexual's incomplete identification with the parent of the same sex. But this in itself is only one aspect of the matter, and in particular there is no recognition of the negative side of same-sex ambivalence as a persisting force in the personality. Healing for the homosexual is not just a matter of meeting unmet needs, but of dealing with the barrier that blocked their fulfilment in the ordinary course of growth and can continue to prevent such fulfilment. Moreover, unmet needs are for love and dependency as well as for identification, and even the identificatory process takes place through the medium of an attachment. The attachment is itself identificatory. Same-sex models may have been available for the homosexual. However, it is not the availability of same-sex models but the ability to be attached to such persons that is crucial in the acquisition of a same-sex identity. Similarly, in the healing process, same-sex relationships will prove an important complement to the healing of memories. The reconstruction of positive mental images through 'faith-imagination' is specially emphasised by Ruth Carter Stapleton. This should be further developed through the actual experience of present-day relationships through which past deficits may be made good. Emotional reconstruction does not depend on mental reconstruction alone, and interpersonal deficits are best dealt with through the medium of renewed interpersonal attachment.

Such attachments for the homosexual need to be with a member of the same sex. Ruth Carter Stapleton, however, speaks of her work with *male* homosexuals. By bringing in the memory of the homosexual's father, or Jesus Christ as a masculine figure, she does introduce a gender-specific element, but can one bypass the gender-specific element in the actual prayer-counsellor? It is God who heals, but he uses us as channels for his healing, and one may not normally expect to bypass his natural laws for human growth. A homosexual may be helped in various ways by a counsellor of the opposite sex, but that person cannot directly help to fulfil same-sex deficits. The full potential of counselling will only be realised when the counsellor is of the same sex as the homosexual. Gender-specificity is not something arbitrary but quite simply the correlation of the solution with the exact nature of the problem. All it means is that a woman cannot be a father, and a man cannot be a mother. Thus, where the problem is specifically a deficit in fathering, a man is required to help; where the problem is specifically a deficit in mothering, it is only a woman who can make this good.

The homosexual condition involves varying degrees of deficit, but in every case there is the same twofold structure and hence the same twofold therapeutic goal of undoing the defensive detachment and meeting unmet needs. Where the deficit is not very marked, the homosexual condition may be readily healed. The greater the defensive barrier, and the more extensive the missing growth, the greater the amount of time and care that will be needed for healing, even though the healing process may well be somewhat accelerated through prayer. In seeking healing, it is important not to pray indiscriminately, but to seek guidance first and at all times. This is especially true if it is not clear how serious the condition is, or if it is clear that the condition is very serious. Having said this, it remains wonderfully true that one can and should pray for the most difficult cases, as well as for others. Prayer can reach the inaccessible and the difficult of access; and, unlike much medication, prayer does not have harmful side-effects![7]

In some instances a lengthy process of healing may be anticipated, quite possibly a matter of some years. Just as ordinary psychological growth takes many years (roughly the first two decades of life), so it is quite reasonable to expect reparative growth to take at least a few years in cases where some significant aspect of growth has been checked since an early age. One cannot expect a child to grow up overnight, or without experiencing sufficient parental care during the long process of growth. Yet this is what is often expected of persons who are psychologically pre-adult even though they have attained adult years. Rapid, if not instant, growth is expected, and this without the provision of relationships, which constitute the normal and necessary means of growth.

But to expect growth to bypass the normal need for time

and for parent-child relationships is certainly unreasonable. Arrested development is no more a 'disease' than being, say, a three-year-old or a nine-year-old is a 'disease'. It is simply a point at which normal growth has not yet been completed. What is pathological is that there should be barriers to such growth which have resulted in pre-adult needs persisting unmet into adult years. No-one would think of praying for a young child to grow up straightaway; nor would one try to 'cure' a three-year-old of being three, since this is not something that needs to be cured. The logic of this is overwhelmingly obvious in such instances, and yet it is precisely this point that tends to be overlooked in questions of psychological healing. Just as it takes years for a young child to grow up, years may be needed for the process of psychological growth when this was checked in a major respect in early life. Time is needed, as are relationships through which pre-adult needs may be satisfied.

For the Christian, this also implies a continuing commitment to prayer. Francis MacNutt takes up Tommy Tyson's phrase 'soaking prayer' to speak of cases 'when we feel that God is asking us to take time to irradiate the sickness with his power and love'.[8] The earlier and the deeper the wound, the longer it will take to heal and the more love and care and prayerful concern will be required. Jim Glennon emphasises the progressive nature of the healing process: 'Healing can come like the growing of a plant; minutely small at first, but in the long run full-grown.'[9] Francis MacNutt speaks of the discovery of the importance of the time element. It is often not a matter of praying just once for a person, as previously thought by some in the healing ministry:

> Prayer for healing is *often a process. It requires time.* There is a *time element* in most healing. ... Praying for chronic ailments of long standing is ... usually a matter of continuing prayer over a long period of time .... For long-term, deep-seated ailments a kind of 'soaking prayer', repeated often, seems to bring the best results.[10]

Likewise, Reginald East: 'See what (God) does and

co-operate in the process of healing if there is not an immediate recovery. Lay hands and pray as many times as necessary.'[11]

Where a psychological deficit is marked, healing may be neither rapid nor easy. But in principle healing is possible for all, whatever the degree of deficit and however ancient the wound and however extensive the missing growth. It is this possibility that we should work towards actualising.

In dealing with the homosexual condition it may help if the persons praying, and the persons prayed for, have some psychological insight into what is involved. In this way one will not be puzzled or taken unawares by some manifestation of the defensive detachment. Nor will one be worried by persisting needs for same-sex love, since such needs, apart from their eroticisation, are quite normal and appropriate. It will also be helpful if the person in question is open and willing for prayer, and it could be a block if they are not. The greatest openness to God's action is when a person has committed their life to Jesus Christ. However, it is clear that Christ himself healed all kinds of people, and that in practice non-Christians can and do receive healing.

A general pattern of prayer for homosexuals has been outlined here. Any given person may also have individual needs, whether or not connected with their homosexuality, that require prayer. In addition, although it is not the subject of this particular study, there is also the possibility of defensive detachment from the parent of the opposite sex, being another area for prayerful concern.

Prevention as well as cure is important, and so we should pray for children at points of vulnerability — both for specific individuals known to us, and as a general area of intercession. Such points of vulnerability would include periods of temporary separation during childhood, and any other occasions on which some strain is placed on the child's attachment to the parent.

Above all, prayer can and should be undertaken by anyone. Agnes Sanford records a minister as saying that 'healing is only answered prayer — and anyone can learn to pray'.[12] All can pray, and prayer is of the essence of healing. And the need for healing — of homosexuality and of other conditions — is so great that all *should* pray. This does not necessitate a special gift of healing. Roy Lawrence states that the important thing is not such a gift, but simply obedience to Christ's command to heal.[13] Francis MacNutt emphasises that the healing ministry should be regarded as *ordinary*[14] and Reginald East states that we can all be used in the ministry of healing.[15]

Such an involvement may well cooperate with conventional psychotherapy, but psychotherapy may not always be necessary and indeed may not always be available. There are only limited specialist resources, and it will be necessary to mobilise widespread help if the need is to be met. Specialists may particularly help within an advisory or supervisory capacity, but people in general may genuinely make a contribution. As parents, men and women are the normal mediators of psychological growth, and the same principle may be taken to apply to reparative psychological growth. *Qua* man or *qua* woman, one can be a mediator of healing. Healing is the general human vocation and capacity.

People in general may pray for the healing of radically incomplete growth as well as for 'easier' cases. Non-specialists can help, and must help. Indeed, it would seem very doubtful that anyone, however professionally qualified, should venture to tackle the more radical cases of defensive detachment and incomplete growth without much prayer.

Love, both in prayer and in relationships, is the basic therapy. A defensive detachment from the same-sex love-source, and consequent unmet needs for love, constitute the homosexual condition. Love is the basic problem, the great need, and the only true solution. If we are willing to seek and to mediate the healing and redeeming love of Christ, then healing for the homosexual will become a great and glorious reality.

NOTES

1. WHAT IS HOMOSEXUALITY?

1 Ovesey (1969) speaks of such problems, but sees them as 'pseudohomosexual'. Here, on the contrary, we would see them as central to the homosexual condition.

2 Most of the psychiatric literature deals with the effects of separation from the mother. It is here suggested that the same principle applies to separation from either parent.

3. THE CHRISTIAN POSITION REASSESSED

1 Suggestions for further reading may be found in the bibliography.

2 Kent Philpott *The Gay Theology*, p.106. See also pp.114, 128, 136.

3 Michael Green, David Holloway and David Watson [Green] *The Church and Homosexuality*, p.19.

4 Ibid. [Green] p.20.

5 Ibid. [Watson] p.136.

6 *The Gay Theology*, p.136.

7 [Green]*The Church and Homosexuality*, p.21.

8 Ibid. p.23.

9 Ibid. p.21.

10 Richard F. Lovelace *Homosexuality and the Church*, p.105.

11 Ibid. p.105.

12 [Holloway] *The Church and Homosexuality*, p.96.

13 Ibid. p.96.

14 Roger Moss *Christians and Homosexuality*, p.31.

15 W. Norman Pittenger *Time for Consent*, p.72.

16 David Field *The Homosexual Way — a Christian Option?*, p.34.

17 John White *Eros Defiled*, p.128.

18 Ibid. p.137. See also [Watson] *The Church and Homosexuality*, p.152.

19 *The Homosexual Way*, p.35.

20 *Eros Defiled*, p.135.

21 *Homosexuality and the Church*, p.111.

22 *The Homosexual Way*, p.44.

23 Ibid. p.45.

24 [Holloway] *The Church and Homosexuality*, p.50.

25 *The Gay Theology*, pp.99,128,136.

26 *Time for Consent*, p.63.

27 Ibid. p.103.

28 [Holloway] *The Church and Homosexuality*, p.75.

29 Ibid. p.107. See also *Homosexuality and the Church*, p.105.

30 *Homosexuality and the Church*, p.103, 149.
31 *The Gay Theology*, p.106.
32 [Green] *The Church and Homosexuality*, p.23.
33 Ibid. p.27.
34 *Time for Consent*, p.103.
35 Ibid. p.9.
36 Ibid. p.103.
37 Ibid. p.75.
38 *Homosexuality   and   the   Church*,   p.144;   *Christians   and
    Homosexuality*, p.7; *The Gay Theology*, p.133; *Time for Consent*,
    p.43.
39 *Eros Defiled*, p.113.
40 Agnes Sanford *Healing Gifts of the Spirit*, p.119.
41 *Eros Defiled*, p.105, 108, 111, 120.

4. HEALING AND PRAYER

 1 [Green] *The Church and Homosexuality*, pp.29-30; *Homosexuality
    and the Church*, p.147; Ruth Tiffany Barnhouse *Homosexuality: a
    Symbolic Confusion*, p.177.
 2 Francis MacNutt *Healing*, p.169.
 3 Ruth Carter Stapleton *The Experience of Inner Healing*, p.21.
 4 Reginald East *Heal the Sick*, p.103.
 5 *Healing*, p.169.
 6 *The Experience of Inner Healing*, p.100.
 7 Cf. Francis MacNutt *The Power to Heal*, p.43.
 8 *The Power to Heal*, p.39.
 9 Jim Glennon *Your Healing is Within You*, p.170. See also pp.63-
    68.
10 *The Power to Heal*, pp.29, 33; *Healing*, p.283.
11 *Heal the Sick*, p.58.
12 *Healing Gifts of the Spirit*, p.62.
13 Roy Lawrence *Christian Healing Rediscovered*, p.93.
14 *The Power to Heal*, p.109.
15 *Heal the Sick*, p.35.

BIBLIOGRAPHY
of works referred to in the text

PSYCHIATRIC LITERATURE
Barnhouse, Ruth Tiffany *Homosexuality: a Symbolic Confusion* Seabury Press (Crossroad Books), New York, 1977.

Bergler, Edmund *Counterfeit-Sex*, Grove Press Inc. and Evergreen Books Ltd, New York and London, 1961.

Bieber, Irving *et al. Homosexuality: a Psychoanalytic Study*, Basic Books Inc., New York, 1962.

Bowlby, John *Separation, Anxiety and Anger*, Hogarth Press, London, 1973.

Fenichel, Otto *The Psychoanalytic Theory of Neurosis*, Routledge & Kegan Paul, London, 1945.

Freud, Sigmund *Psycho-analytic Notes on an Autobiographical Account of a Case of Paranoia* (The Schreber Case), Standard Edition, XII, 1911.

Green, Richard *Sexual Identity Conflict in Children and Adults*, Duckworth, London, 1974.

Ovesey, Lionel *Homosexuality and Pseudohomosexuality*, Science House, New York, 1969.

Socarides, C. W. *The Overt Homosexual*, Grune & Stratton, New York and London, 1968.

Stoller, Robert J. *The Transsexual Experiment*, Hogarth Press, London, 1975.

Storr, Anthony *Sexual Deviation*, Pelican Books, 1974.

Walinder, Jan *Transsexualism*, Scandinavian University Books, Goteborg, 1967.

HOMOSEXUALITY: THE CHRISTIAN DEBATE
Field, David *The Homosexual Way — a Christian Option?*, Inter-Varsity Press, Leicester, 1979.

Green, Michael, Holloway, David and Watson, David *The Church and Homosexuality*, Hodder & Stoughton, London, 1980.

Lovelace, Richard F. *Homosexuality and the Church*, Lamp Press, London, 1979.

Moss, Roger *Christians and Homosexuality*, Paternoster Press , Exeter, 1977.

Philpott, Kent *The Gay Theology*, Logos International, Plainfield, N.J., 1977.

Pittenger, Norman *Time for Consent*, SCM Press, London (Third edition, revised and enlarged, 1976).

White, John *Eros Defiled*, Inter-Varsity Press, Leicester, 1978.

See also

Bailey, Derrick Sherwin *Homosexuality and the Western Christian Tradition*, Archon Books (Shoe String Press), Hamden, Conn., 1975.

Macourt, Malcolm, ed. *Towards a Theology of Gay Liberation*, SCM Press, London, 1977.

Scanzoni, Letha and Mollenkott, Virginia Ramey *Is the Homosexual my Neighbour?*, SCM Press, London, 1978.

HEALING

East, Reginald *Heal the Sick*, Hodder & Stoughton, London, 1977.

Glennon, Jim *Your Healing is Within You*, Hodder & Stoughton, London, 1979.

Lawrence, Roy *Christian Healing Rediscovered*, Kingsway Publications, Eastbourne, 1976.

MacNutt, Francis *Healing*, Bantam, New York, 1977. *The Power to Heal*, Ave Maria Press, Notre Dame, Indiana, 1977.

Sanford, Agnes *Healing Gifts of the Spirit*, Arthur James Ltd, Evesham, 1966.

Stapleton, Ruth Carter *The Experience of Inner Healing*, Hodder & Stoughton, London, 1978.